Pupil Book 2

Composition Skills

Authors: Abigail Steel and Chris Whitney

HarperCollins
PUBLISHERS
Since 1817

William Collins' dream of knowledge for all began with the publication of his first book in 1819. A self-educated mill worker, he not only enriched millions of lives, but also founded a flourishing publishing house. Today, staying true to this spirit, Collins books are packed with inspiration, innovation and practical expertise. They place you at the centre of a world of possibility and give you exactly what you need to explore it.

Collins. Freedom to teach.

Published by Collins
An imprint of HarperCollins*Publishers*
The News Building
1 London Bridge Street
London
SE1 9GF

Browse the complete Collins catalogue at
www.collins.co.uk

British Library Cataloguing in Publication Data A Catalogue record for this publication is available from the British Library

Publishing Director: Lee Newman
Publishing Manager: Helen Doran
Senior Editor: Hannah Dove
Project Manager: Emily Hooton
Authors: Abigail Steel and Chris Whitney
Development Editor: Robert Anderson
Copy-editor: Ros and Chris Davies
Proofreader: Tanya Solomons
Cover design and artwork: Amparo Barrera and Ken Vail Graphic Design
Internal design concept: Amparo Barrera
Typesetter: Jouve India Private Ltd
Illustrations: Beatriz Castro, Aptara and QBS
Production Controller: Rachel Weaver

Printed in Great Britain by Martins the Printers

Acknowledgements

The publishers wish to thank the following for permission to reproduce content. Every effort has been made to trace copyright holders and to obtain their permission for the use of copyright materials. The publishers will gladly receive any information enabling them to rectify any error or omission at the first opportunity.

HarperCollins Publishers Ltd for an extract on page 4 from *Brown Bear and Wilbur Wolf* by Sarah Parry, copyright © Sarah Parry, 2012. Reproduced by permission of HarperCollins Publishers Ltd; Hachette Children's Group for an extract on page 6 from *First Fairy Tales: Puss in Boots* by Margaret Mayo. First published in the UK by Orchard Books, an imprint of Hachette Children's Group, Carmelite House, 50 Victoria Embankment, London EC4Y 0DZ. Reproduced with permission; Usborne Publishing Ltd for the story on page 8 'The Fox and The Crow' from *Illustrated Stories from Aesop*. Reproduced by permission of Usborne Publishing, 83–85 Saffron Hill, London EC1N 8RT, UK, www.usborne.com, copyright © 2013 Usborne Publishing Ltd; HarperCollins Publishers Ltd for an extract on page 10 from *Pompeii The Lost City* by Fiona Macdonald, copyright © Fiona Macdonald, 2012. Reproduced by permission of HarperCollins Publishers Ltd; Usborne Publishing Ltd for an extract on page 12 from *First Encyclopedia of History*. Reproduced by permission of Usborne Publishing, 83–85 Saffron Hill, London EC1N 8RT, UK, www.usborne.com, copyright © 2011 Usborne Publishing Ltd; HarperCollins Publishers Ltd for an extract on page 16 from *How Does it Work?* by Sylvia Karavis and Gill Matthews, copyright © HarperCollins Publishers Ltd, 2005. Reproduced by permission of HarperCollins Publishers Ltd; Curtis Brown Group Ltd for the poem on page 20 'My Name Is...' by Pauline Clarke published in *The Booktime Book of Fantastic First Poems*, copyright © Pauline Clarke, 1905. Reproduced with permission of Curtis Brown Group Ltd, London on behalf of The Beneficiaries of the Estate of Pauline Clarke; Caroline Sheldon Literary Agency Ltd for the poem on page 22 'Don't Call Alligator Long-Mouth Till You Cross River' by John Agard, copyright © 1986 by John Agard. Reproduced by kind permission of John Agard c/o Caroline Sheldon Literary Agency Ltd; and HarperCollins Publishers Ltd for an extract on page 46 from *Collins Primary Focus: Introductory Pupil Book* by John Jackman and Wendy Wren, copyright © John Jackman and Wendy Wren, 2013; HarperCollins Publishers Ltd for the extract on pages 25–26 from *The Stone Cutter* by Sean Taylor, copyright © 2005 Sean Taylor; the extract on pages 27–28 from *The Journey of the Humpback Whale* by Andy Belcher, copyright © 2012 HarperCollins Publishers Ltd; the extract on pages 30–31 from *The Digestive System* by Harriet Blackford, copyright © 2012 HarperCollins Publishers Limited; the extract on pages 33–35 from *Oliver* by Hilary McKay, copyright © 2012 Hilary McKay; the extract on page 36 from *How to Make Pop-up Cards* by Monica Hughes, copyright © 2005 Monica Hughes; the extract on pages 40–41 from *Caterpillar* by Wendy Cope, copyright © 2010 Wendy Cope; the extract on pages 43–44 from *Tig in the Dumps* by Michaela Morgan, copyright © 2005 Michaela Morgan; the extract on pages 49–50 from *The Pot of Gold* by Julia Donaldson, copyright © 2006 Julia Donaldson; the extract on pages 52–53 from *The Boy with Wings* by Simon Cheshire, copyright © 2015 Simon Cheshire; the extract on pages 55–56 from *Brown Bear and Wilbur Wolf* by Sarah Parry, copyright © 2012 Sarah Parry. Reproduced by permission of HarperCollins Publishers Ltd.

The publishers would like to thank the following for permission to reproduce photographs: p.11 Fotos593/Shutterstock, p.27 Flickr Select/Alexander Safonov/Getty Images, p.27 (b) © Andy Belcher, p.30 Camille Tokerud/Getty Images, p.36 © HarperCollins Publishers Ltd, p.42 graphic-line/Shutterstock.

MIX
Paper from
responsible sources
FSC www.fsc.org **FSC** C007454

Contents

Personal stories (1)

From 'Brown Bear and Wilbur Wolf' by Sarah Parry and Judy Musselle

Brown Bear was hungry. He had been asleep all winter. He came out of his den and stretched. The snow had melted and the grass was green. Brown Bear looked around him and sniffed the air, but he couldn't smell anything.

He went into the forest to look for berries, but he couldn't smell anything.

He went to the river to look for fish, but he couldn't smell anything.

'I've lost my smell,' he said sadly to himself. 'How will I find any food?'

He lay down in a meadow by the river and tried to remember all his favourite smells – the smell of trees, the smell of new grass, the smell of apples and leaves, of berries, of rain and snow.

Get started

Draw pictures of the things that
Brown Bear remembered and label them.

1. the trees and grass
2. the apples and leaves
3. the berries
4. the rain and snow

Try these

Copy and complete the sentences using your own ideas.

1. Brown Bear felt …
2. The weather was …
3. Brown Bear went to …
4. The problem was …

Now try these

1. What is Brown Bear thinking about at the end of the story? Write a sentence.
2. Draw a picture of Brown Bear looking sad or worried. Add a caption.
3. What happens next? Write the next part of the story.
4. Plan a short story about a character looking for something they have lost.

Fairy tales

From 'Puss in Boots' by Margaret Mayo

Once upon a time, in a windmill on top of a hill, there lived an old man and his three sons. When the old man died, he left the windmill to the eldest son, a donkey to the second and a cat called Puss to the third.

The youngest son was upset. He wanted to have the windmill or the donkey. 'I am fond of you, Puss,' he said, as he stroked the cat, 'but you're not very useful. Except for catching mice!'

Get started

Copy the sentences and complete them using words from the fairy tale.

1. Once upon a time, there was a
_____ on top of a hill.

2. In the _____ there lived an
_____ _____ and his
three sons.

3. The eldest son was given the _____ .

4. The second son was given a _____ .

5. The youngest son was given a _____ .

Try these

Write the next part of the fairy tale by copying and completing the sentences.

1. The youngest son went to live in …

2. He got a job as …

3. The cat stayed with him and they …

4. One day he was asked to give the cat to …

5. Then an amazing thing happened …

Now try these

1. Draw a picture of the third son looking disappointed about getting the cat.

2. Write a sentence to explain how the son felt about Puss.

3. What are the son and Puss saying in your picture? Add speech bubbles to your picture.

4. Plan your own story about Puss. Draw and label pictures or write a few sentences.

Traditional tales (1)

From 'The Fox and the Crow'

'How delicious!' thought Crow, looking at a picnic left lying in the shade. 'So much food ... And no one's around ...'

Her beady black eye was caught by a piece of juicy meat lying just out of reach. 'Oh!' thought Crow. 'It's so tempting. If I swoop down fast enough,' she decided, 'I can get it, I'm sure.'

And she went for it, darting down, a blur of black feathers. Snap, snap, went her sharp beak, and then she headed back into the woods, flapping her fringed wings, a very proud thief.

Get started

Copy the sentences and complete them using words for different kinds of food.

1. 'How delicious! I can see _____ ,' thought Crow.

2. 'Oh yum! I can smell _____ ,' said Crow.

3. 'Wow! There's _____ ,' exclaimed Crow.

4. 'Scrumptious! A big juicy _____ ,' declared Crow.

5. 'That _____ looks tasty!' cackled Crow.

Try these

Answer the questions to create a story opening for 'The Fox and the Crow'.

1. When did the story happen?

2. Where did the story happen?

3. What was the weather like in the story?

4. What time was it in the story?

5. Who was there at the start of the story?

Now try these

1. Write a sentence about Crow taking some more food.

2. Think of a new animal character. Draw a picture of them talking to Crow.

3. What are they saying? Add speech bubbles to your picture.

4. Plan your own short story about an animal that takes some food. Draw and label a picture or write some sentences.

Information writing

Volcano danger

Vesuvius began to erupt in AD 79. A mighty earthquake shook the ground. Clouds of ash hid the sun and the sky went dark. The people of Pompeii were terrified.

The eruption lasted for two days. A massive explosion hurled rocks into the sky. Red-hot lava poured out of the volcano. Deadly clouds of burning gas rolled over Pompeii. The air was full of falling ash, which looked like black snow.

Get started

Copy the sentences and decide if they are facts or opinions. Then write 'fact' or 'opinion'.

1. Vesuvius began to erupt in AD 79.

2. I think it was noisy.

3. I think it was very scary.

4. The eruption lasted for two days.

5. The explosion hurled rocks into the sky.

Try these

Read the text and write a sentence to answer each question.

1. What is the text about?

2. What is the first fact in the text?

3. What was the first thing that happened when Vesuvius erupted?

4. How long did the eruption last?

5. How many sentences are there in the text?

Now try these

1. Draw a picture of Vesuvius erupting. Label the different parts of your picture.

2. Draw a picture of the people of Pompeii watching Vesuvius erupt.

3. What are the people of Pompeii saying? Add speech bubbles to your picture.

4. Plan ideas for an information text about your school. Draw and label a picture or write some sentences.

Reports

Ancient Egyptians

The Ancient Egyptians were farmers who lived along the banks of the Nile. They used water from the river to help them grow food. The Egyptians were ruled by a powerful king called a pharaoh.

Pharaohs and pyramids

Some pharaohs were buried inside huge, stone pyramids on the edge of the desert. The pharaoh's body was placed in a secret room in the middle of the pyramid.

Get started

Copy the sentences and decide if they are true or false. Then write 'true' or 'false'.

1. Reports can use headings.

2. Reports can use topic-specific words.

3. Reports are always about Ancient Egypt.

4. Reports need very long sentences.

5. Reports never use full sentences.

Try these

Read the report and answer the questions.

1. What is the report about?

2. There are two headings. What are they?

3. Who were the Ancient Egyptians?

4. What does the second section of the report focus on?

5. Find three facts. Write them down.

Now try these

1. Draw a picture of the Ancient Egyptians building a pyramid. Label your picture.

2. What else would you like to know about the Ancient Egyptians? Write a heading for a third section of the report.

3. Write five key words for a report on Ancient Egypt.

4. Plan ideas for a report on a topic you have been learning about in school. Draw and label a picture or write some sentences.

Simple instructions

Papier-mâché house

You will need lots of newspaper, a small cardboard box, a fork, a bowl, one cup of flour, one and a half cups of water, a teaspoon of salt, and a quarter of a cup of white glue.

Clear a large area and cover the table with newspaper. Put the water and the flour into the bowl, and mix together with the fork until it is runny. Mix in the salt and the glue. Tear newspaper into strips. Dip a strip completely into the paste, then remove excess paste by running the strip between your thumb and finger. Lay the strip on the cardboard box. Do the same with more strips until the box is completely covered. Leave the box to dry, then cover it again with new strips. Let it dry again and cover it one more time with strips. Then your house is ready for painting!

Get started

Copy and complete the instructions using your own imperative (bossy) verbs.

1. _____ the things you will need.

2. _____ your hands.

3. _____ the items on the table.

4. _____ the instructions carefully.

5. _____ the table afterwards.

Try these

Write one instruction for part of each task.

1. washing hands
2. getting dressed
3. making breakfast
4. making a birthday card
5. going to bed

Now try these

1. What do we call the bossy verbs that are used in instructions?

2. Draw and label a diagram to show how to tidy up a mess.

3. Draw and label a diagram to show how to peel an orange.

4. Write your own set of instructions to explain how to do one of the following:

   • dance the hokey cokey

   • make a paper aeroplane

   • draw an animal (you choose what animal)

Simple explanations

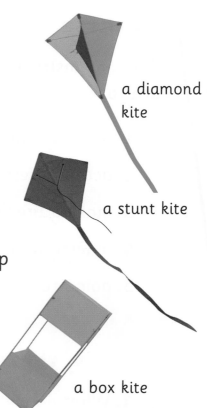

a diamond kite

a stunt kite

a box kite

How does a kite work?

Kites come in many shapes and sizes, but they all use the wind to fly.

A kite is a frame covered in light material. It has a thin, strong piece of string tied to the frame. As you hold up a kite, air lifts it up so that it can fly.

Get started

Copy the sentences and decide if they are true or false. Then write 'true' or 'false'.

1. All kites are diamond shaped.

2. All kites are blue.

3. Kites come in many shapes and sizes.

4. Only some kites use the wind to fly.

5. Kites have a frame covered in light material.

Try these

Copy and complete the sentences using your own ideas.

1. A kite is a …

2. It is best to fly a kite when …

3. If you are in a busy park, …

4. Your string might …

5. Flying a kite is …

Now try these

1. Draw and label a diagram of a kite.

2. Write a sentence to explain what a pencil is.

3. Write a sentence to explain what a book is.

4. Write a short explanation to help people understand what a bicycle is and how to ride it.

Information texts

A. Write a fact file or information text about the village or town where you live. Use a template like this to help you.

Title:	
Opening sentence or sentences:	
Information box 1	Information box 2
Information box 3	Information box 4
Diagrams or illustrations	

Writing stories

B. It is Kim's birthday. She's seven years old and is hoping for a present from a special person. Write the story of her day. Use a template like this to help you.

Title: The surprise birthday present
Opening sentence or sentences:
Now write about what happened next. Was there a present or not?
How did the day end for your character?

Instruction texts

C. Write the instructions for how to play a playground game. Remember to use command verbs. You may illustrate each step as you write it. Use a template like this to help you.

Title: Instructions for playing _____	
What you need:	
1	2
3	4
5	6

Poetry: Wordplay

'My Name Is ...'
My name is Sluggery-wuggery
My name is Worms-for-tea
My name is Swallow-the-table-leg
My name is Drink-the-sea
My name is I-eat-saucepans
My name is I-like-snails
My name is Grand-piano-George
My name is I-ride-whales
My name is Jump-the-chimney
My name is Bite-my-knee
My name is Jiggery-pokery
And Riddle-me-ree,
and ME.

Pauline Clarke

Get started

Copy the sentences and decide if they are true or false.
Then write 'true' or 'false'.

1. The poem repeats the words 'My name is'.

2. The poem uses hyphens to join words together.

3. The poem uses some made-up words.

4. The poem is thirteen lines long.

5. The poem does not rhyme.

Try these

Copy and complete the phrases using your own words.

1. My name is _____ window

2. My name is _____ paper

3. My name is _____ handbag

4. My name is _____ spiders

5. My name is _____ centipede

Now try these

1. What do you think Sluggery-wuggery looks like? Draw a picture.

2. What would you say to Sluggery-wuggery if you met him?

3. Write two silly sentences that start with 'My age is ...'.

4. Write a poem like the one about Sluggery-wuggery about one or several of your toys. Start each line of your poem with 'My toy is ...'

Poetry: Alligator

'Don't Call Alligator Long-Mouth till You Cross River'

Call alligator long-mouth

call alligator saw-mouth

call alligator pushy-mouth

call alligator scissors-mouth

call alligator raggedy-mouth

call alligator bumpy-bum

call alligator all dem rude word

but better wait

till you cross river.

John Agard

Get started

Copy the sentences and decide if they are true or false.
Then write 'true' or 'false'.

1. The poem is about a chimpanzee.

2. The poem repeats the words 'call alligator'.

3. 'dem' is a mistake made by the poet.

4. 'dem' shows the poet speaks with an accent.

5. All of the insults are about the alligator's eyes.

Try these

Copy the phrases and complete them using words for different
kinds of animal.

1. call _____ wide-mouth

2. call _____ short-legs

3. call _____ razor-claws

4. call _____ wobble-nose

5. call _____ messy-paws

Now try these

1. Draw and label a picture of the alligator.

2. What might the alligator say? Add a speech bubble to your picture.

3. Write two 'call alligator' sentences that are nice rather than insulting.

4. Write your own fun poem about a different animal using the style of 'Don't Call Alligator Long-Mouth till You Cross River'

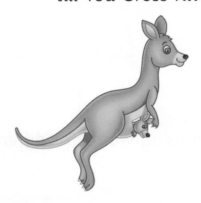

Get started

Copy the sentences and decide if they are true or false. Then write 'true' or 'false'.

1. The poem is about a chimpanzee.

2. The poem repeats the words 'call alligator'.

3. 'dem' is a mistake made by the poet.

4. 'dem' shows the poet speaks with an accent.

5. All of the insults are about the alligator's eyes.

Try these

Copy the phrases and complete them using words for different kinds of animal.

1. call _____ wide-mouth

2. call _____ short-legs

3. call _____ razor-claws

4. call _____ wobble-nose

5. call _____ messy-paws

Now try these

1. Draw and label a picture of the alligator.

2. What might the alligator say? Add a speech bubble to your picture.

3. Write two 'call alligator' sentences that are nice rather than insulting.

4. Write your own fun poem about a different animal using the style of 'Don't Call Alligator Long-Mouth till You Cross River'

Stories from another culture

From 'The Stone Cutter' by Sean Taylor and Serene Curmi

A poor stone cutter chipped at a rock. His hammer went TACK and his chisel went TOCK.

Then a rich man walked past, in his rich clothes. 'I'm just a poor stone cutter,' the stone cutter said. 'I'd rather be a rich man instead.'

And he became a rich man.

Then the emperor rode past with his servants dressed in blue and gold. 'I'm just a rich man,' the stone cutter said. 'I'd rather be the emperor instead.'

And he became the emperor.

Then the sun came out. It was grander and more powerful than any emperor.

Get started

Copy the sentences and complete them using words from the story.

1. First of all the poor stone cutter wanted to be a
   _____ _____.

2. Then he wanted to be an _____.

3. The emperor was dressed in _____
   _____ _____.

4. The sun was more _____ than any emperor.

Try these

Answer the questions to create the rest of the story.

1. Why was the stone cutter not happy?

2. What did he want to be?

3. What do you think he will want to be next?

4. Will he ever be happy?

Now try these

1. Write the sentence that comes next in the story.

2. Think of three other things that the poor stone cutter might want to be.

3. Write some sentences using your ideas about what he might want to be.

4. Add the last sentence to your story. It should say what happened to the poor stone cutter in the end.

Information writing: Fact files

From 'The Journey of the Humpback Whale' by Andy Belcher

Humpback whales are mammals, not fish. This means they can't breathe under water. Humpbacks have two big nostrils (blowholes) on the top of their heads and must come to the surface to breathe.

Adult humpbacks can stay under water for up to 45 minutes and dive to a depth of 180 metres. They're called humpbacks because they arch their backs when they dive.

Humpbacks are known as 'acrobats of the sea' because they leap out of the water. This is called breaching.

Each humpback has different white, grey and black patterns under its tail. Although humpbacks are very big, they still face dangers like strong currents, storms, getting caught in fishing nets or being hit by boats.

Get started

Copy the sentences and complete them using words from the information about humpback whales.

1. Humpback whales are _____, not fish.

2. Humpbacks have _____ _____
   _____ _____ on the top of their heads.

3. Adult humpbacks can stay under water for _____
   _____ _____ _____.

4. They are called humpbacks because …

5. Humpbacks are very big but they still face dangers like …

Try these

Read the text again and write a sentence to answer each question.

1. How do humpbacks get their name?

2. What do you know about the patterns under a humpback's tail?

3. How deep can they dive?

4. What does 'breaching' mean?

5. Information texts often have technical vocabulary like 'breaching' or 'currents'. Here are some more: mammals, blowholes. What do these last two words mean? Use a dictionary to help you.

Now try these

1. Draw a spider diagram and add the facts you know from the text about humpback whales.

2. Now choose another animal and make a list of facts you know about it.

3. Draw another spider diagram and add the facts to this.

4. Write some information sentences about your chosen animal using the facts from your spider diagram.

Whales

Explanation writing: Healthy eating

From 'The Digestive System' by Harriet Blackford

Why do we eat different types of food?

Food and drink have to be broken up into very small pieces for our bodies to use. We call this digestion and it takes place in our digestive system. There are many different types of food. Foods like meat, fish, nuts, eggs, cheese and milk are important for growth. Energy for playing and working comes from foods such as potatoes, rice, pasta, bread and cereals. We also get energy from fatty and oily food such as cooking oil, butter, nuts and seeds. These foods are important for our health too. We need to eat a variety of food including fresh fruit and vegetables to make sure our bodies grow and stay healthy. This is called a balanced diet.

Get started

Copy the sentences and complete them using words from the information about healthy eating.

1. Food and drink have to be broken up into _____ _____ _____ for our bodies to use.

2. We call this _____.

3. Foods like meat, fish, nuts, eggs, cheese and milk are important for _____.

4. Energy for playing and working comes from foods such as …

5. We also get energy from _____ and _____ _____ such as cooking oil, butter, nuts and seeds.

Try these

Read the text again and write a sentence to answer each question.

1. What is the text about?

2. Why do we need to eat a variety of food?

3. Which foods are good for growth?

4. Which foods are good for playing and working?

Now try these

1. Write a sentence about your favourite food and when you ate it last.

2. Write some sentences explaining why we need to eat a balanced diet.

3. Draw a labelled diagram to show what would be in a healthy eating lunchbox.

4. Write a note telling parents what should be in their child's lunchbox.

Stories set long ago

From 'Oliver Twist' by Charles Dickens, retold by Hilary McKay and Rupert Van Wyk

Nearly 200 years ago, a baby was born. His name was Oliver Twist.

Oliver was born in a workhouse. In those days when the poorest of poor people had nothing left to keep them alive – no home, no money, no family, no hope – they were sent to the workhouse. People of all ages were sent there to work hard making things like sacks or clothes.

Oliver's workhouse was run by a man called Mr Bumble and it was one of the worst. People starved to death in that place and Mr Bumble was pleased when they did. Dead people didn't need dinners. In Mr Bumble's workhouse, the meals never changed. Gruel was served three times a day. Gruel was a sort of watery porridge – it didn't fill you up and it didn't make you grow.

When Oliver was nine years old, he was about the size of a boy of six and he was as hungry as a starving tiger. So were all the other boys in the workhouse. They were hungrier than they could bear and, one day, they made up their minds to ask for more gruel.

Oliver walked up to the fat man who gave out the gruel and he said, 'Please sir, I want some more.'

Mr Bumble and all his helpers went wild with rage. They pushed poor Oliver into the cellar while they thought about what to do with him.

Get started

Copy the sentences and complete them using words from the story.

1. Nearly 200 years ago, a baby was born. His name was

   _____ _____ .

2. He was born in a _____ .

3. Oliver's workhouse was run by a man called

   _____ _____ .

4. Gruel was a sort of _____ _____ .

5. They made up their minds to ask for _____

   _____ .

Try these

Read the text again and write sentences to answer each question.

1. Why were people sent to the workhouse?

2. What did they do there?

3. What food was Oliver given to eat?

4. Why did he ask for more?

Now try these

1. Copy the picture of the boys eating gruel. Draw some speech bubbles and write what you think they are saying or thinking in the speech bubbles.

2. Copy the picture of Oliver asking for more gruel. In a speech bubble write the words he said.

3. In another speech bubble, write the words that Mr Bumble said to Oliver after this.

4. Write some sentences telling the story of what you think happened to Oliver next. Start with the last line of the text: 'They pushed poor Oliver into the cellar while they thought about what to do with him.'

Instructions

From 'How to Make Pop-up Cards' by Monica Hughes

Making the spring for a pop-up card

Things you will need

- two strips of paper of different colours
- a small stapler
- a glue stick
- a pair of scissors

Making the spring

1. Pick up the two strips of paper.
2. Put the end of one strip on top of the other strip to form an L shape.
3. Staple the strips together.
4. Fold the bottom strip over the top strip and press it down.
5. Fold the bottom strip over the top strip again.
6. Follow steps 4 and 5 again and again.
7. Stop halfway and check that your spring is still a square shape.
8. Carry on folding until you reach the end of the strips.
9. Glue down the last fold and press it hard.
10. Cut off any extra paper at the end of the spring.

Well done! You are ready to add the spring to your card.

Get started

1. When was the last time you had to follow a set of instructions?

2. Write a few sentences explaining why you needed them and if and how they helped.

Try these

1. Write down the imperative word that gives the command in each step of 'Making the spring'.

2. Explain why instructions should be written in order.

3. Sometimes writers use 'time' words like 'then', 'next' or 'finally' to help put the instructions in order. Choose three instruction sentences from the text and copy them out, adding a 'time' word to them. For example, 'First, pick up the two strips of paper.'

Now try these

1. Write a set of instructions for making a fruit salad. Make sure that you have included 'Things you will need'.

2. Check that you have used imperative verbs and have numbered the instructions.

3. Sometimes writers use a flowchart to show step-by-step instructions. A flowchart can have diagrams or pictures of the things you need and what to do.

   Draw a flowchart for making the fruit salad.

4. Proofread your work, checking for clear step-by-step instructions and correct spelling and punctuation.

Review unit 2

Explanation texts

A. Draw a simple flowchart to show the different stages in the life of a butterfly. Write sentences to go with each part of the life cycle.

Writing poems

B. Write a rhyming poem about children arriving at school in the morning that follows the pattern shown. The first one has been done for you. Use a template like this to help you.

Title: Arriving at school
In come the children two by two
They have many fun things to do!
In come the children three by three
_____ (Add your line here to rhyme with the line above.)
In come the children four by four
_____ (Add your line here to rhyme with the line above.)
In come the children five by five
_____ (Add your line here to rhyme with the line above.)

Planning longer stories

C. Plan a story set in an old house. You need to choose two characters and it must include some treasure. Who will be in my story? What will happen in your story? Where and when will it happen? How will it end? Use a template like this to help you.

Title:	
Who are your characters?	Where and when will it happen?
What will happen in your story?	How will it end?

Poetry: Animal rhymes

Caterpillar

Once a chubby caterpillar

Sat upon a leaf,

Singing, 'Eat, eat and be merry –

Life is very brief.'

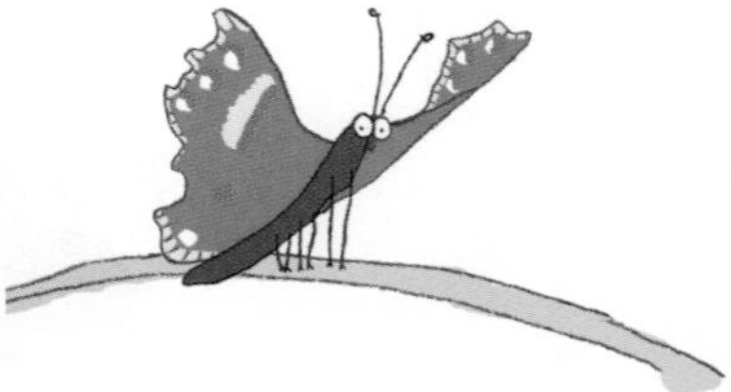

Soon he lost his appetite

And changed his merry tune.

He started spinning, hid himself

Inside a hard cocoon.

And he was still and quiet there –

Day after day went by.

At last it cracked and he emerged,

A gorgeous butterfly.

He spread his brown and crimson wings

And warmed them in the sun,

And sang, 'Now I must see the world —

My life has just begun.'

Wendy Cope

Get started

1. Write a sentence about what has happened to the caterpillar by the end of the poem.

Try these

1. Use a dictionary to help you explain the meaning of the following words:

   a) appetite   b) cocoon   c) emerged   d) crimson

2. Use these words in sentences of your own.

3. Look at how the poet has made the poem rhyme. Which lines in each stanza rhyme? List the words that rhyme.

4. Look at the first stanza. Why did the caterpillar think that life was 'very brief'?

5. In the same stanza, why is he called a 'chubby' caterpillar?

Now try these

1. Draw pictures of the life cycle of a frog.

2. Copy the poem below and add the rhyming word to the first stanza. Lines 2 and 4 rhyme.

Once a tiny tadpole

Inside a blob of jelly

Began to grow and grow and grow

With the food inside its _____.

Egg Mass

Adult frog

Tadpole

Froglet

Tadpole with Legs

3. Copy the next stanza and write the rhyming word at the end of line 4.

The tadpoles swam deep within the pond –

They were no longer eggs.

At first the back and then the front

They found they had some _____.

4. Write the last verse of this poem. It should be about the froglet turning into a frog.

Narrative

From 'Tig in the Dumps' by Michaela Morgan

Tig had heard every word Miss Simmons had said. She'd said: 'Think of all the lovely books you've read in school. Look!' Miss Simmons waved her hand at a display of books and posters. 'You could be a character from any of these books. You could be a detective ... or a hobbit ... or a superhero.'

All that day, Miss Simmons went on about Book Day. 'You could dress up as a pirate. Or you could be my favourite character, Stig of the Dump. You all enjoyed 'Stig of the Dump' when we read it, didn't you? It's about a boy who finds a real Cave Boy in a pit, remember?'

At playtime everyone decided which characters they were going to be. Tig hoped nobody was going to remember the costume he wore last year. His mum had gone to lots of trouble to make his costume. But she'd made one tiny mistake.

Get started

Copy the sentences and add the missing words from the story.

1. Tig had heard every word _____ _____ had said.

2. Miss Simmons waved her hand at a display of _____ and posters.

3. 'You could be a _____ or a hobbit or a _____.'

4. All that day, Miss Simmons went on about _____ _____.

5. At _____ everyone decided which characters they were going to be.

Try these

Read the text again and then answer these questions.

1. Why does Miss Simmons ask the children to think of all the books they've read this year?

2. What could the prize be for the best costume?

3. What is the name of the main character in the book you are reading at the moment?

4. Do you think Tig is looking forward to Book Day this year?

Now try these

Write the rest of the story by writing sentences to answer these questions.

1. What costume does Tig decide to wear?

2. What problem could happen to Tig on Book Day?

3. How does it get sorted?

4. How does the story end?

Non-chronological report

Budgerigars and canaries make good pets

Where they came from

The first budgerigars (or budgies as they are called) were brought from Australia, and canaries came from the Canary Islands.

Song

Budgies make a loud squawking sound but can usually learn to talk. The canary is the best singer of all the birds that are kept as pets.

Handling your pet

Budgies can be handled more easily than canaries. In fact, they seem to like sitting on a finger or shoulder. They also like to fly around the room, so make sure they can't fly into or onto a fire.

Feeding

Both budgies and canaries eat seeds as well as some green plants. Both have strong bills for cracking hard seeds for the kernels. Birds need clean water all the time.

Get started

Copy the sentences and decide if they are true or false. Then write 'true' or 'false'.

1. The first budgerigars were brought from Australia.
2. Budgies don't make any noise.
3. Both budgies and canaries only eat meat.
4. They do not need clean water.

Try these

Read the text again and answer the following questions.

1. What are the subheadings of the four main parts of the report?
2. Why are there four sections in the report?
3. What verb tense do we use when writing a report?
4. What else could you include to give more information to the reader?

Now try these

1. Choose an animal to write a non-fiction report about. Find out some facts.

2. Use these subheadings to organise your writing:

   - What it looks like

   - Where it lives

   - What it eats

   - Other interesting facts

3. Check that your report uses the present tense for verbs, for example: Giant pandas live in China.

4. Add an illustration or labelled diagram.

Traditional tales (2)

From 'The Pot of Gold' by Julia Donaldson

Sandy and Bonny kept sheep. The two of them were always arguing.

One evening, they were busy arguing when there was a tap at the door. There on the doorstep stood a little man. He wore a green hat and a ragged green coat. His green shoes had holes in the toes.

'Can I stay here for two nights?' he asked.

'Yes,' said Sandy.

'No,' said Bonny.

'I can pay,' said the little man. He took two gold coins out of his pocket.

'Well?' he asked. 'Can I stay?'

'Yes!' said Sandy and Bonny. For once they agreed about something.

They took him to his room.

'Good night, and good luck!' said the little man.

Bonny laughed. 'We never have any luck,' she said. But she was wrong.

The next day, Sandy was on the hill with the sheep when he saw a big pile of stones. 'That's funny,' he said. 'I can see something gleaming.'

Get started

Copy the sentences and add the missing words from the story.

1. Sandy and Bonny kept _____.

2. The two of them were always _____.

3. One evening, they were busy arguing when there was a ___ __ ___ _____.

4. There on the doorstep stood a _____ ___.

5. He wore a _____ _____ and a _____ _____ _____.

Try these

Now read the story again and answer the questions.

1. Why did Sandy and Bonny say that the man could stay?

2. Were they being kind or greedy?

3. What do you think was gleaming in the pile of stones?

4. Read the following blurb for the story 'The Pot of Gold':

   Sandy and Bonny were always arguing and nothing ever went right for them. But one day a little man came to stay. Would he really change their luck?

   Continue the blurb by writing a sentence about what you think might happen next in the story.

Now try these

1. Draw a picture of what you think Sandy will do next.

2. Write a sentence under this to show what is happening.

3. Think about how the story will end. Draw three more pictures that show what happens to Sandy and Bonny and the little man.

4. Add some sentences under each picture.

Myths

From 'The Boy with Wings' by Simon Cheshire and Dylan Coburn

The maze had been built by Daedalus himself, on the orders of the king. The maze was called the Labyrinth, and nobody who'd ever entered it had found a way out. Except for one man! A Greek hero called Theseus had killed the Minotaur, and had escaped from the Labyrinth using a ball of string. Then he'd run way from Crete, taking King Minos's daughter Ariadne with him. The king was furious with Daedalus for helping Theseus by giving him the string. Daedalus and his son were sad and frightened in the maze.

'Don't you know the way out of here, Dad?' said Icarus. 'You built this place.'

'It's so large', said Daedalus, 'that, without a map, even I can't escape from it.'

Get started

Copy the sentences and decide if they are true or false. Then write 'true' or 'false'.

1. The maze had been built by Daedalus himself, on the orders of the king.
2. The maze was called the Labyrinth.
3. Many people had found a way out of the maze.
4. A Greek hero called Theseus killed the Minotaur.
5. Daedalus and his son were happy to be in the maze.

Try these

Now read the story again and answer the questions.

1. Who told Daedalus to build the maze?
2. What was Daedalus's son called?
3. How did Daedalus help Theseus to escape from the maze?
4. Why were they sad and frightened in the maze?
5. How do you think they will escape?

Now try these

1. Draw a picture showing how you think they escape from the maze.

2. Write a sentence under this to show what is happening.

3. Add speech bubbles to show what they are saying to each other.

4. Think about how the story will end. Draw two more pictures to show what happens after they escape from the maze.

5. Add some sentences under each picture. Check that you have correctly used capital letters and full stops.

Personal stories (2)

From 'Brown Bear and Wilbur Wolf' by Sarah Parry and Judy Musselle

Brown bear lay down. He was all alone and was still hungry.

Wilbur Wolf came out of the forest. He was old and tired and had been looking for food all winter. He saw Brown Bear in the field and walked slowly towards him. 'Maybe Brown Bear can tell me where to find some food,' Wilbur said to himself.

Brown Bear was too tired and hungry to get up when Wilbur came near, so Wilbur wasn't scared. They lay in the tall grass, and Brown

Bear explained that he'd lost his smell.

'Without my smell, how will I find any food?' Brown Bear asked.

Wilbur shrugged. 'I'm old and weak,' he said. 'How will I catch any food?'

Get started

Copy the sentences and decide if they are true or false. Then write 'true' or 'false'.

1. Brown Bear was not hungry.
2. Wilbur Wolf came out of the shops.
3. He was old and tired and had been looking for food all winter.
4. They lay in the tall grass, and Brown Bear explained that he'd lost his pencil.

Try these

Now read the story again and answer the questions.

1. Why was Brown Bear hungry?
2. Why couldn't Wilbur Wolf catch any food?
3. Why wasn't Wilbur Wolf scared of Brown Bear?
4. What is Wilbur Wolf worried about?

Now try these

1. What will Brown Bear say next? Draw a speech bubble and write in it the words he says to Wilbur Wolf.
2. Brown Bear has lost his smell. What is the problem for Wilbur Wolf?
3. Draw a picture to show the first thing they might do to help each other.
4. Plan and write a story about two animals who help each other and become friends.

Non-chronological reports

A. Write a report about a bird of your choice. Research information and then decide how to present the information.

Instructions

B. Write a set of instructions for making a sandwich of your choice. Use a template like this to help you.

Name of sandwich:
What you need for the sandwich:
How to make the sandwich:

Planning longer stories

C. Research a Greek myth of your choice. Summarise it in pictures as in a story map and add sentences under each picture to explain what is happening. Use a template like this to help you.

Title:	
1	2
3	4
5	6